M000164580

THE ROYAL HORTICULTURAL SOCIETY

PLANT
NOTEBOOK

Illustrations from the Royal Horticultural Society's Lindley Library

FRANCES LINCOLN

Frances Lincoln Limited
4 Torriano Mews
Torriano Avenue
London NW5 2RZ
www.franceslincoln.com

The Royal Horticultural Society Plant Notebook
Copyright © Frances Lincoln Limited 2004

British Library cataloguing-in-publication data
A catalogue record for this book is available from the British Library

Printed in China
ISBN 0-7112-2351-3
First Frances Lincoln edition 2004

COVER
A hand-retouched chromolithograph of a tree peony, a variety of
Paeonia suffruticosa, illustrated by Louis-Aristide-Léon Constans
in *Paxton's Flower Garden* (1850– 51)

TITLE PAGE
A coloured drawing of tulip 'May Blossom' by Lewis Cording (1970s)

CONTENTS

A GROWING SOCIETY

Throughout its history, the Royal Horticultural Society has inspired people to discover new and interesting plants and encouraged an interest in gardening. This RHS Plant Notebook is designed to help you to keep notes on your own personal discoveries.

With its spectacular flower shows, world-class gardens and the highest standards in advice, science and education, the RHS is at the heart of gardening today. To become a member, all you need is an interest in gardening. One of the many benefits of membership is free access to our Garden Advice Service covering such queries as where to buy and how to grow plants, plant identification, pests and diseases and garden products. For more information please call our membership hotline on 0845 130 4646 or log onto our website: www.rhs.org.uk.

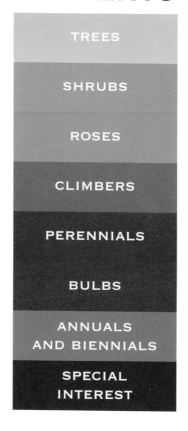

TREES

A coloured drawing of the English oak, *Quercus robur*,
by Daphne Brotherston (1996)

PLANT NAME	WHERE SEEN

SUPPLIER	PLANTING POSITION

PLANT NAME	WHERE SEEN

PLANT NAME	WHERE SEEN

SUPPLIER	PLANTING POSITION

SUPPLIER	PLANTING POSITION

SUPPLIER	PLANTING POSITION

SHRUBS

A hand-coloured engraving of the common gum cistus,
Cistus ladaniferus, from the third volume of the *Icones plantarum
medico-oeconomico-technologicarum* of Ferdinand Bernhard Vietz (1806)

PLANT NAME	WHERE SEEN

SUPPLIER	PLANTING POSITION

PLANT NAME	WHERE SEEN

SUPPLIER	PLANTING POSITION

PLANT NAME	WHERE SEEN

SUPPLIER	PLANTING POSITION

PLANT NAME	WHERE SEEN

SUPPLIER	PLANTING POSITION

PLANT NAME	WHERE SEEN

SUPPLIER	PLANTING POSITION

PLANT NAME	WHERE SEEN

SUPPLIER	PLANTING POSITION

PLANT NAME	WHERE SEEN

SUPPLIER	PLANTING POSITION

ROSES

A coloured engraving of *Rosa* 'York and Lancaster'
from *Les Roses* (1817–24) by Pierre-Joseph Redouté

PLANT NAME	WHERE SEEN

SUPPLIER	PLANTING POSITION

PLANT NAME	WHERE SEEN

SUPPLIER	PLANTING POSITION

PLANT NAME	WHERE SEEN

SUPPLIER	PLANTING POSITION

SUPPLIER	PLANTING POSITION

PLANT NAME	WHERE SEEN

SUPPLIER	PLANTING POSITION

CLIMBERS

A coloured drawing of 'Clematis purpurea', probably a form
of *Clematis viticella*, by Margaret Meen (1789)

PLANT NAME	WHERE SEEN

SUPPLIER	PLANTING POSITION

PLANT NAME	WHERE SEEN

SUPPLIER	PLANTING POSITION

PLANT NAME	WHERE SEEN

SUPPLIER	PLANTING POSITION

PLANT NAME	WHERE SEEN

SUPPLIER	PLANTING POSITION

PLANT NAME	WHERE SEEN

SUPPLIER	PLANTING POSITION

PERENNIALS

A coloured engraving of aquilegias from Jane Loudon,
The Ladies' Flower-Garden of Ornamental Perennials (1840)

PLANT NAME	WHERE SEEN

SUPPLIER	PLANTING POSITION

PLANT NAME	WHERE SEEN

SUPPLIER	PLANTING POSITION

PLANT NAME	WHERE SEEN

SUPPLIER	PLANTING POSITION

PLANT NAME	WHERE SEEN

SUPPLIER	PLANTING POSITION

PLANT NAME	WHERE SEEN

SUPPLIER	PLANTING POSITION

PLANT NAME	WHERE SEEN

SUPPLIER	PLANTING POSITION

PLANT NAME	WHERE SEEN

SUPPLIER	PLANTING POSITION

PLANT NAME	WHERE SEEN

BULBS

A coloured drawing of three tulips –
'Golden Harvest', 'May Blossom' and 'Glacier' –
by Lewis Cording (1970s)

SUPPLIER	PLANTING POSITION

PLANT NAME	WHERE SEEN

SUPPLIER	PLANTING POSITION

PLANT NAME	WHERE SEEN

PLANT NAME	WHERE SEEN

SUPPLIER	PLANTING POSITION

ANNUALS
AND
BIENNIALS

A coloured engraving of zinnias from Jane Loudon,
The Ladies' Flower-Garden of Ornamental Annuals (1842)

PLANT NAME	WHERE SEEN

SUPPLIER	PLANTING POSITION

PLANT NAME	WHERE SEEN

PLANT NAME	WHERE SEEN

SUPPLIER	PLANTING POSITION

PLANT NAME	WHERE SEEN

SUPPLIER

PLANTING POSITION

SPECIAL
INTEREST

A hand-coloured engraving of auricula 'Bertle's Royal Sportsman'
by James Sowerby from his *Florist's Delight* (1789–91)

PLANT NAME	WHERE SEEN

SUPPLIER	PLANTING POSITION

PLANT NAME	WHERE SEEN

SUPPLIER	PLANTING POSITION

PLANT NAME	WHERE SEEN

SUPPLIER	PLANTING POSITION

PLANT NAME	WHERE SEEN

SUPPLIER	PLANTING POSITION

PLANT NAME	WHERE SEEN

SUPPLIER	PLANTING POSITION

NOTES